Australian States *and Territories*

NORTHERN TERRITORY

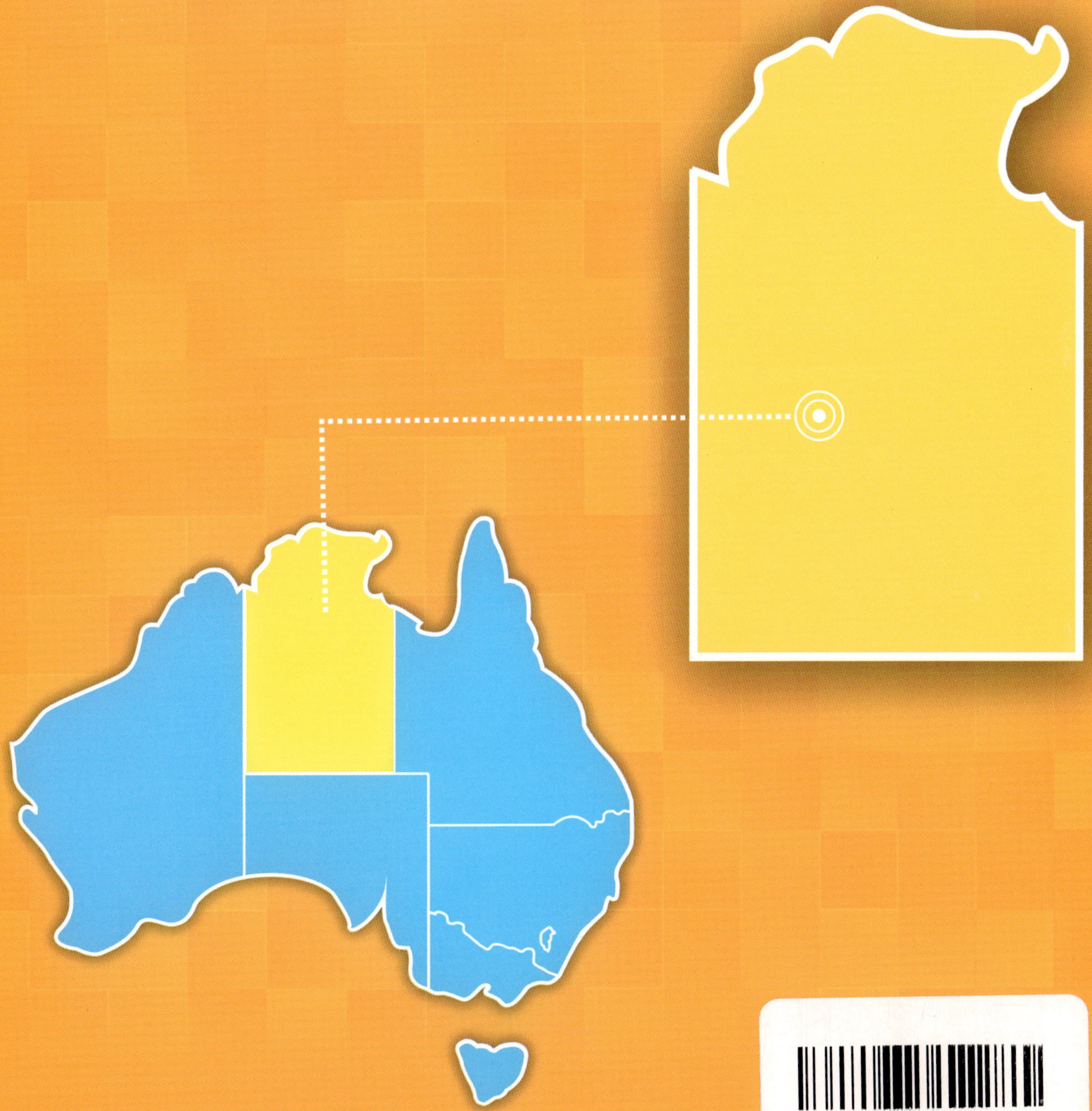

Linsie Tan

Redback Publishing
Suite 6, 13a Narabang Way,
Belrose NSW 2085
Australia

Reprinted 2025

ISBN 978-1-925630-42-8

Author: Linsie Tan
Editor: Jane Hinchey
Original illustrations © Redback Publishing 2018
Originated by Redback Publishing

Acknowledgements
We would like to thank the following for permission to reproduce photographs: National Library of Australia - Group of Aboriginal men of the Yolngu language group standing with H.E. Boote next to a group of Aboriginal women sitting, Elcho Island, Northern Territory, ca. 1923, PIC Album 364 #PIC/14912/1, Prime minister Gough Whitlam pours soil into the hand of Gurindji Traditional Land Owner Vincent Lingiari at Wattie Creek, Northern Territory, 16 August 1975, Mervyn Bishop, PIC/16014/30, Street scene in a residential area of Darwin after Cyclone Tracy, December, 1974, Alan Dwyer, PIC/8827/22, Three unidentified men, one an Afghan camel driver, standing next to a camel train, John Flynn, PIC P850 17/14 LOC Cold store PIC AIM 36/1537, John Gould, Schomynv, Bahnfrend, Squiresy92, Stephen Michael Barnett.

A catalogue record for this book is available from the National Library of Australia

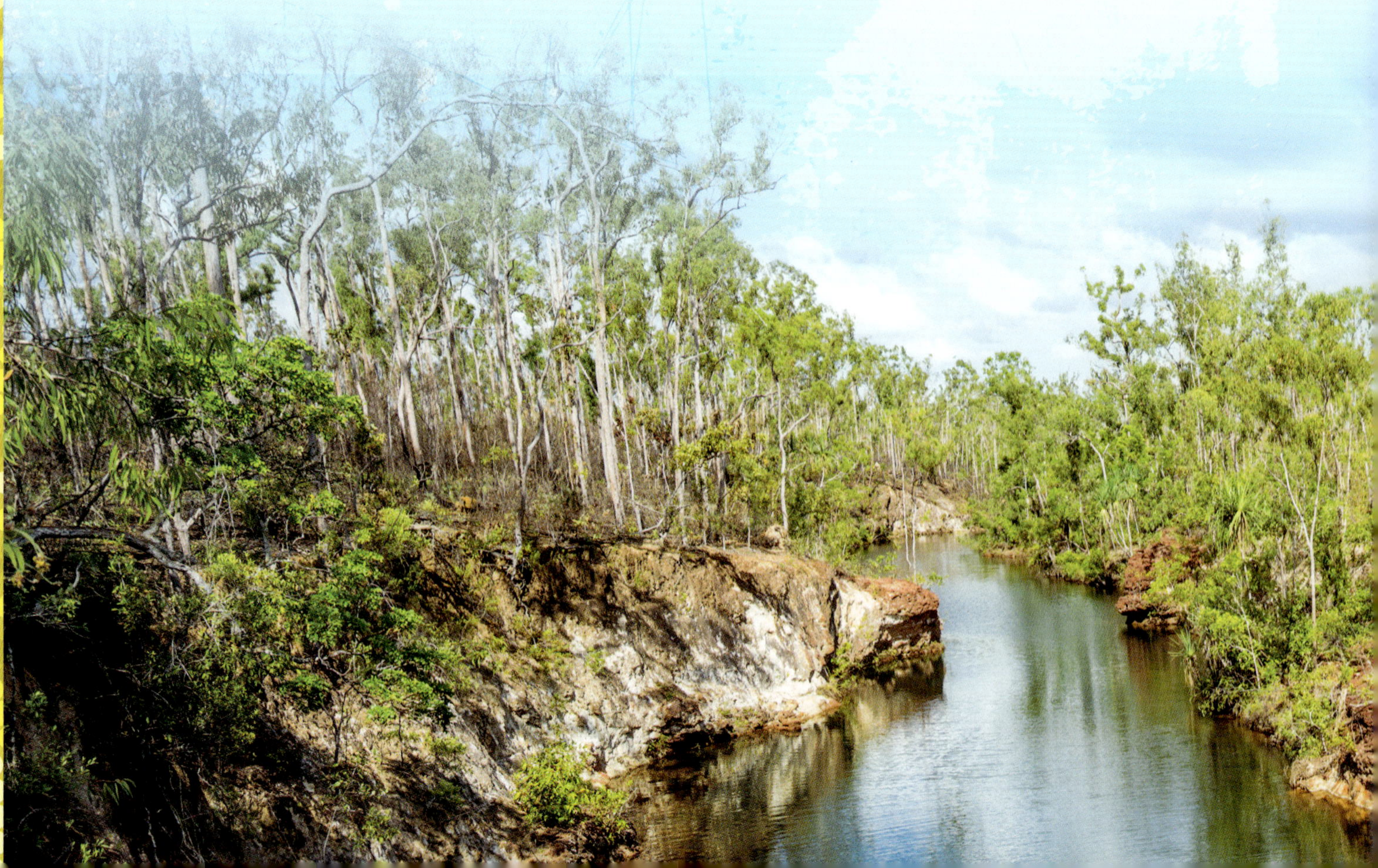

CONTENTS

Some words are shown in red, **like this**.
You can find out what they mean by
looking in the glossary.

Geography of the Northern Territory

The Northern Territory is bounded by Western Australia, South Australia and Queensland. The nearest country is Indonesia to the north across the Arafura Sea.

Regional Towns

The Northern Territory has five main towns that act as the supply and service centres for extensive areas surrounding them. They are Darwin, Alice Springs, Katherine, Tennant Creek and Nhulunbuy.

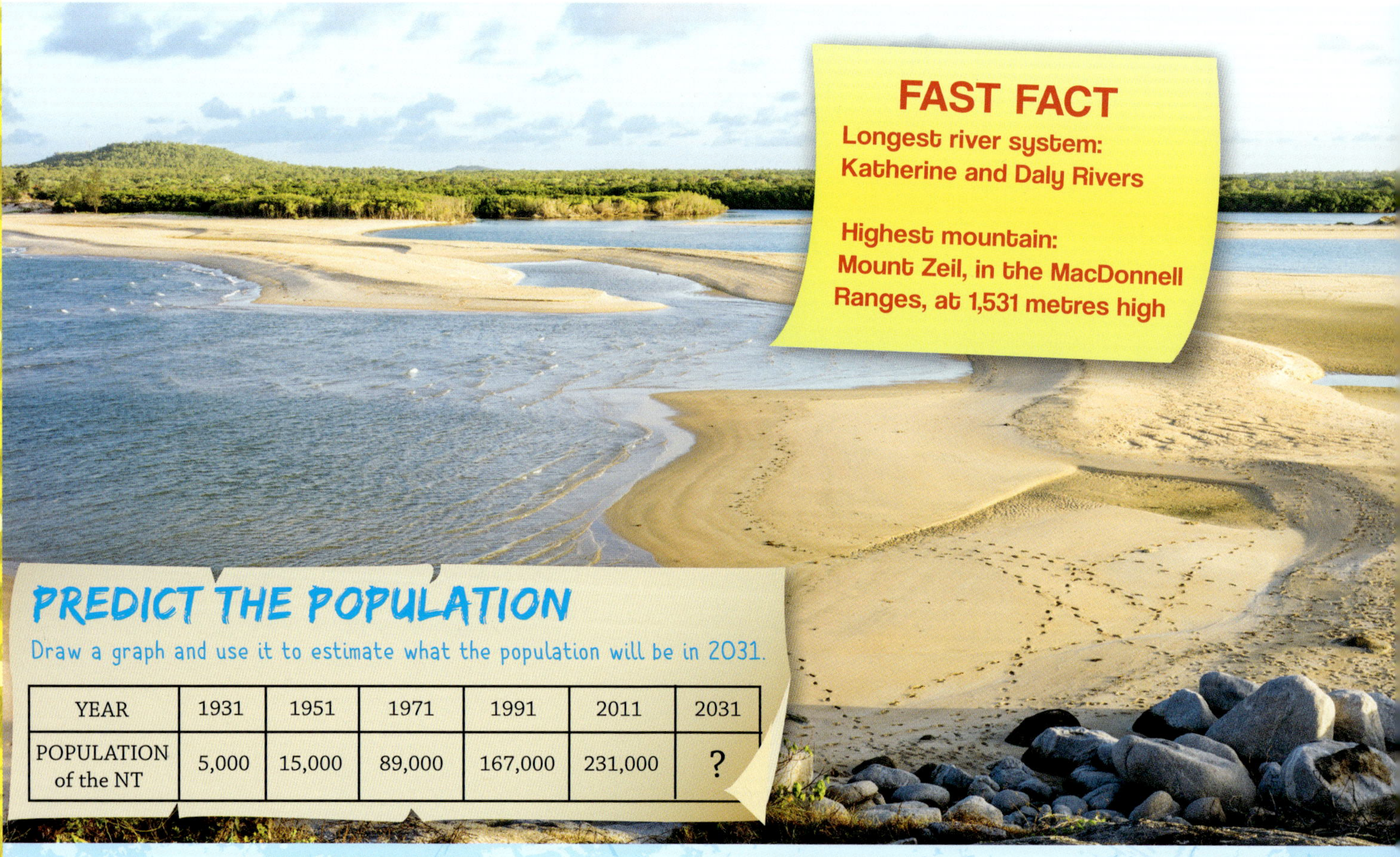

FAST FACT

Longest river system: Katherine and Daly Rivers

Highest mountain: Mount Zeil, in the MacDonnell Ranges, at 1,531 metres high

PREDICT THE POPULATION

Draw a graph and use it to estimate what the population will be in 2031.

YEAR	1931	1951	1971	1991	2011	2031
POPULATION of the NT	5,000	15,000	89,000	167,000	231,000	?

Climate

There are two distinct climatic regions in the Northern Territory. In the north, the climate is tropical, with a dry and wet season and an annual monsoon that brings heavy rains. The southern part of the Northern Territory is very arid, with infrequent rainfall. Dry creeks and riverbeds that receive monsoonal rainfall can suddenly fill and create a hazard for vehicles and campers. Cyclones in the north regularly sweep across the Northern Territory, threatening human lives, causing floods and destroying wildlife habitats and buildings.

Finke River and the MacDonnell Ranges

The Finke River is an extremely ancient river system, even older than the surrounding MacDonnell Ranges, which were formed in a geologic event about 300 million years ago.

WEATHER

- Highest recorded temperature in the Northern Territory 48.6 °C at Finke in 1960
- Lowest recorded temperature in the Northern Territory -7.5 °C at Alice Springs in 1976

Deserts of the Northern Territory

Simpson Desert

Famed for its long, parallel sand dunes, the Simpson Desert is home to a variety of wildlife, including the bilby and the hopping mouse. These animals survive by hiding from the heat during the day and coming out to feed at night. Feral camels in the desert are the descendants of camels released after the Overland Telegraph Line was completed in 1872.

Tanami Desert

Now under the custodianship of the Warlpiri and Kartangururru-Kurintji Aboriginal people, the Tanami desert is a vast sanctuary for plants and animals adapted to a desert habitat.

Islands of the Northern Territory

Groote Eylandt

The traditional owners of Groote Eylandt are the Anindilyakwa people. The local economy depends on tourism, mining, fishing and Anindilyakwan arts and crafts. There are about forty smaller islands nearby, many of which are uninhabited.

Tiwi Islands

This island group includes Bathurst and Melville Islands. They are 100 kilometres north of Darwin and are home to the Tiwi people. Non-residents need a permit to visit the Tiwi Islands.

Aboriginal History of the Northern Territory

Aboriginal people have lived in Australia for at least 60,000 years. The continent of Australia was once connected to landmasses to the north, and people could travel easily across dry land and the shallow seas. Aboriginal people developed complex societies and ways of life, and their culture depends on having strong spiritual connections to the land.

Trade With the Macassans

Before British settlement, Aboriginal people from the Northern Territory area traded with Macassans, who were sailors from Indonesia and other countries to the north. Rock paintings by Aboriginal artists show Indonesian sailing ships. There are also archaeological remains of campsites used by the Macassan traders, who were seeking the sea cucumber, a prized food in southeast Asia.

European Settlers and the Aboriginal Nations

Darwin was founded on the land of the Larrakia or saltwater people. As the settlers claimed more land, their cattle and sheep replaced native food animals, and they colonised areas that had been in traditional ownership for thousands of years.

Aboriginal Nations in the Northern Territory

Yolngu
Warlpiri
Pitjantatjara
Arrernte
Luritja
Gurindji

THINK ABOUT IT

These are only a few of the Aboriginal nations in the Northern Territory. How many more can you name?

Archaeology

Archaeologists look for the remains of human activity to investigate the history of the people who were responsible for creating them. All of these types of archaeological sites are found in the Northern Territory:

- shell middens
- quarries for ochre
- stone arrangements
- rock art

Historians and archaeologists also use:

- oral history
- old documents
- radiocarbon dating
- DNA evidence

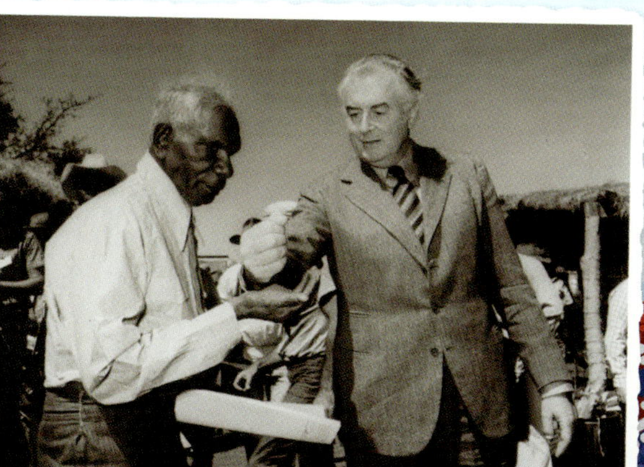

1966 - The Wave Hill Strike

A strike by Aboriginal workers on the Wave Hill cattle station in the Northern Territory developed into a demand for land rights. In 1972, the land was officially returned to its Aboriginal owners, the Gurindji people, by Prime Minister Whitlam.

WORD FILE

colonise - to settle in a new land and impose a new culture on the people living there
traditional ownership - the Aboriginal land ownership system
contemporary - modern

Aboriginal Art of the Northern Territory

Contemporary Aboriginal artists use the x-ray style and dot paintings to create works of art on bark and on canvas. This art from the Northern Territory is a vibrant, living extension of art styles that have an ancient heritage. Traditionally, the images were painted on rock walls and on bark, and the symbolic art style was used for ceremonial body decoration and for temporary works made in the sand.

The magnificent dot paintings produced by the artists at Papunya have enthralled art markets around the world. These artists are credited with the birth of the modern Aboriginal art movement, which has resulted in some paintings selling for millions of dollars.

Aboriginal art from the Northern Territory is a spiritual expression by artists who represent the oldest continuous human culture in the world.

Place Names

The Northern Territory was the first government to use dual-naming for places. Using this system, place names are created using a combination of an Aboriginal and another name. Uluru / Ayers Rock was the first example of dual naming in the Northern Territory.

FAST FACT

Aboriginal people make up about 30% of the population of the Northern Territory. This is the highest proportion in any Australian state or territory.

History of Settlement in the Northern Territory

The British government established a settlement on the north coast of the Australian continent to discourage the Dutch from claiming the land first. Dutch explorers had been visiting the waters of the Torres Strait and Arafura Sea since the 1600s.

Explorers and Settlers Timeline

1600s Macassan traders from the islands and countries to the north traded with the Aboriginal people living on the coastal areas of the Northern Territory.

1623 Dutch explorer William Jootszoon van Colster sighted the coast.

1644 Dutchman Abel Tasman sailed along the coast though the Torres Strait.

1803 Matthew Flinders circumnavigated Australia and landed in Arnhem Land.

1839 Captain Wickham aboard the HMAS Beagle explored the waters of Port Darwin. The famous naturalist, Charles Darwin, was one of his passengers.

1845 Ludwig Leichhardt reached the Port Essington military post after leaving the Darling Downs in Queensland. He and his men were sick and exhausted after their arduous journey.

1861 to 1862 John McDouall Stuart explored the continent from south to north. His successful expeditions and reports on the agricultural value of the land he found encouraged the colonial government to consider a permanent northern port.

1869 After several failed attempts at settlement, Britain finally established the town of Palmerston, later to become the city of Darwin.

THINK ABOUT IT

The first five attempts by the British to establish a township on the Northern Territory's coast all failed. Why do you think this happened?

Darwin

1869 - George Goyder was sent by the South Australian government to establish a settlement at the site of Darwin. The purpose was to make the area suitable for settlers to pasture their livestock. Goyder named the settlement Palmerston.

1871 - Gold was discovered at Pine Creek.

1871 - The undersea telegraph cable link with London came ashore at Palmerston, making it an important location for international communication. The only other way to send messages overseas was by letters sent in ships powered by sails or steam.

1911 - Palmerston was renamed Darwin, after Charles Darwin.

The Bombing of Darwin

In 1942, during the Second World War, Darwin was bombed by Japanese fighter planes, resulting in destruction of the city and many deaths. This was the largest enemy attack on Australia during the war.

Left: Australian postal stamp showing the bombing of Darwin during World War II, 1942

Right: Street scene in a residential area of Darwin after Cyclone Tracy, December, 1974

Cyclone Tracy

Cyclone Tracy was Australia's most destructive cyclone in recorded history. Striking Darwin on Christmas Day 1974, the cyclone flattened buildings and killed many people.

Multicultural Darwin

Darwin is a multicultural city. The large community of people with Chinese heritage has a long history in the area. Chinese came in the 1800s to help build the Overland Telegraph Line and the discovery of gold in the Northern Territory brought many seeking their fortune.

The Portuguese-Timorese community in Darwin grew in size after the refugees from violence in East Timor arrived there after 1999. Greek-Cypriot, Filipino and Indian people have also made their home in the Northern Territory, along with people from many other countries.

Darwin Botanic Gardens

Established in the 1880s, the Darwin Botanic Gardens contain a collection of tropical plants and trees. The Wesleyan Methodist Church is the oldest building in Darwin and it has been reconstructed within the grounds of the Botanic Gardens.

Afghan Cameleers

The Afghan cameleers came to central Australia in the 1800s, along with their camels, to provide a transport and delivery service. Although they were called Afghans, the men actually originated from a number of Middle Eastern countries and from India.

The camels carried building materials for the railway from Adelaide to Alice Springs, and for the telegraph line. With no local shops, many of the settlers depended on the Afghans to supply them with their household needs. The camels were better suited to the desert conditions than horses or bullocks, and the cameleers who owned them were skilled in training and looking after their animals.

As motor vehicles became more popular and affordable, and after the railway line was completed, the Afghans and their camel delivery services were no longer needed. Most of the remaining camels were released into the wild. Some of the men returned home, while others settled in Australia. Their proud descendants can be found throughout the areas where their ancestors used to work. Their mosques and cemeteries are reminders of the vital service the Afghan cameleers provided for the settlement of central Australia.

Alice Springs

Alice Springs is located on the traditional lands of the Arrernte Aboriginal people.

1862 - The first European to find the area was the explorer, John McDouall Stuart, who was mapping a route to the northern coast of the Australian continent.
1871 - The surveyor of the route for the new Overland Telegraph Line found a waterhole in the area and called it Alice Springs.
1933 - The town at the end of the Overland Telegraph Line was originally called Stuart, but was renamed Alice Springs.
1887 - Gold was discovered at Arltunga near Alice Springs.

School of the Air

The extreme remoteness and the small populations of towns across the Northern Territory meant that children did not always have the opportunity to go to school. They received their lessons by post, which was often delayed for weeks during the wet season.

In 1951, the first School of the Air was established in Alice Springs to broadcast by radio to children in isolated, outback areas. By 1956, the School of the Air was also broadcasting from Broken Hill to children in NSW. Since there was often no electricity supply on outback farms, children used pedal powered radios to contact the teachers. These old radios are now replaced with satellite communication and web cameras.

Transport in the Northern Territory

Before European Settlement

The first methods of transport used by Aboriginal people in the Northern Territory were walking and paddling canoes. Canoes were made of bark or from hollowed out logs, and they were used for fishing and to cross rivers and harbours. 'Canoe trees' are important reminders of this early technology.

Aboriginal men in large dug out canoes, 1934

Roads

The large areas and small population of the Northern Territory mean that roads are still dirt tracks in many regional locations, and are subject to flooding during the monsoon. In the deserts, sudden flooding can make roads unusable.

The Stuart Highway connects Darwin with Adelaide, the Barkly Highway runs to north Queensland and the Victoria Highway to Western Australia.

Royal Flying Doctor Service

John Flynn set up a medical service to the outback using aircraft to fly doctors to their patients. Concerned that there was no way to call the doctor in the case of an emergency, he helped design a radio transmitter which could be used to call for a home visit using Morse code. Pedal power was used to generate the electricity needed to run the radios and they were first distributed in 1926. The radio base for the Flying Doctor Service was established in Alice Springs.

Airports

The first airport at Darwin was built in 1919. During the Second World War, the airport attracted Japanese bombing raids. Today, RAAF Base Darwin shares the runways with the Darwin International Airport traffic.

There are also airports at Alice Springs and Tennant Creek. The solar energy project at Alice Springs airport provides the majority of the airport's energy needs.

Road Trains

Road trains are trucks pulling multiple trailers. They provide the transport services that railways offer in the more populated parts of Australia, carrying cattle, ore, fuel and many other bulk goods. Although they are common in the Northern Territory, road trains are rarely seen in the southern states. Tourists from these areas who are unused to sharing the road with a road train need to be cautious about attempting to overtake a vehicle that might be as long as a suburban block. The Northern Territory government specifies safe routes that road trains should use.

Port Darwin

With no roads or railways linking Darwin with the rest of Australia, early residents of the Top End relied on ships to transport goods and travellers to the rest of Australia.

Port Darwin is now a shipping port with facilities for container ships, cruise ships and bulk ore carriers. The Adelaide to Darwin railway line ends at Port Darwin, where there are facilities for loading bulk ore shipments from miners who export overseas.

Railway

A railway linking Adelaide with Alice Springs was completed in 1929, but it was not until 2003 that the tracks were finally extended northward to Darwin. The passenger train linking Darwin with Adelaide is called The Ghan, after the Afghan cameleers who helped to build the railway line. A trip on The Ghan is one of the world's great train journeys. There is no commuter railway service in the Northern Territory's cities, and no rail links between towns not on the Ghan railway line.

WORLD HERITAGE SITE

KAKADU NATIONAL PARK

Kakadu National Park is one of two World Heritage Sites in the Northern Territory. Located about 240 kilometres east of Darwin, Kakadu is the largest national park in Australia. Some of the ancient rocks in the park date back to over 2,500 million years ago. Noted for the diversity of its flora, fauna and landscapes, Kakadu encompasses mangroves, coastal plains, sandstone cliffs, wetlands and forest, each with its own array of wildlife, some of which is not found anywhere else.

Wildlife

Plants and animals in Kakadu have evolved adaptations to allow them to survive in the park's varied habitats.

- The green plum has waxy leaves to reduce water loss during the dry season.
- Eucalypt trees have a deep root system to allow them to access sources of water underground.
- The Kakadu plum loses its leaves in the dry season to conserve water.
- The Cooktown ironwood produces a poison that deters animals and termites from eating it.
- Resurrection grasses appear to be dead in the dry season but will revive quickly after rain.
- Snake-necked turtles burrow into the mud as the water dries up.

The Importance of Mangroves

Mangroves provide a vital habitat for many species of aquatic and land animals. They also stabilise the coastline, reducing damage to delicate ecosystems from storms and waves. Mangroves have evolved special ways to deal with having their root system submerged in salt water, a condition that would kill other trees. These adaptations include:

- Having some roots that grow upwards into the air instead of down into the soil.
- Having the ability to pump salt out of their leaves and roots.

Escarpments

The sandstone cliffs in Kakadu are called escarpments. They are up to 300 metres high. During its long history, the land that is now Kakadu was once submerged under a sea, with the cliffs at Twin Falls and Jim Jim forming the shoreline. Nourlangie Rock and Ubirr were once islands in this ancient sea. The stony escarpment is now the location of the waterfalls, gorges and rock art sites which make Kakadu such a popular tourist destination. While the surface of the stony area may be dry and hot, the deep gorges and pools provide microclimates that support a lush variety of plants and the animals that feed on them.

Coastline and Tidal Flats

The coastline of Kakadu provides nurseries for many species of fish, which spend their juvenile stages in the safety of the mangrove swamps, before heading out to the open sea when they have grown larger. The mangroves also provide nesting places for birds during the wet season. The beaches offer egg-laying sites for flat-back turtles and the sea-grass beds just off the shore support dugongs. Crocodiles also live in these northern parts of Kakadu, and attacks on people near waterways have occurred.

Wetlands

About thirty species of migratory birds visit the Kakadu wetlands each year. They have come from Siberia, China and Japan and depend on the presence of a pristine environment for their continued existence. Australia has agreements with the governments of China and Japan to ensure that the breeding grounds of these migratory birds are preserved.

Ranger Uranium Mine

The Ranger Uranium Mine is within the boundaries of Kakadu. In consultation with the Aboriginal custodians of the land, the mine management will restore the site as their mining operations are concluded.

Bininj Mungguy People

Kakadu is on the traditional lands of the Bininj Mungguy Aboriginal people. In their Dreaming, the wonders of Kakadu were created by their ancestral and spirit figures.

Warramurrungundji, Mother of the Earth, created the waterways and wildlife. She taught her children how to live on the land and, when she rested after this task, she became a large rock. This is now her Dreaming site.

The Rainbow Serpent is usually a female spirit in the Kakadu Dreaming. She is always present in the land, and likes water and quiet areas. If disturbed, she can create natural disasters to show her displeasure.

The rock art of Kakadu is mostly found in the rocky escarpment. Some of the older art was created by ancestral spirits to teach future generations about laws.

Archaeologists have dated the rock art to 20,000 years ago, and human habitation to 50,000 years ago. The Bininj Mungguy people trace their ancestry to the time of the creation of the land by the ancestral spirits.

Six Seasons

Kakadu's traditional custodians have six seasons, based on the climate, the landscape and the behaviour of the animals in it.

December - March:	Gudjewg (monsoon season)
April:	Banggerreng (stormy season)
May - June:	Yegge (cool season)
June - August:	Wurrgeng (cold season)
August- October:	Gurrung (hot and dry season)
October - December:	Gunumeleng (pre-monsoon season)

WORD FILE

escarpments - cliffs at the edge of a plateau
microclimate - the climate in a very small area

WORLD HERITAGE SITE

ULURU - KATA TJUTA NATIONAL PARK

Uluru

The Yankunytjatjara and Pitjantjatjara Aboriginal people are the traditional custodians of Uluru and Kata Tjuta.

Uluru is over 300 metres high and is thought to extend two kilometres underground. It measures more than nine kilometres around the base. The nearest town to Uluru is Alice Springs, 450 kilometres away. To accommodate the thousands of tourists who come to see and experience Uluru, the service centre of Yulara was built nearby.

The first European to find Uluru was William Gosse in 1873. He named it Ayers Rock.

Rock Art

The rock art around Uluru was painted using ochre and other natural substances. The same symbols are repeated across the region and include circles, U shapes, animal tracks, dots and paths. The paintings were made for spiritual purposes and to teach the next generations of people about law and the ancestral creation spirits.

Mala (Rufous-Hare Wallaby)

The ancestors were the Mala people and their descendants have a responsibility to protect the Mala. This wallaby was extinct on the Australian mainland, but a group of them has been reintroduced to the area around Uluru and is now thriving.

Handing Back Uluru

On 26th October 1985, Uluru was handed back to its traditional custodians by the Australian government. The national park is now jointly managed by the Australian Parks and Wildlife Service and its Aboriginal owners.

Kata Tjuta

Kata Tjuta is a group of dome shaped rocks about fifty kilometres away from Uluru, within the Uluru - Kata Tjuta National Park The name means 'many heads' in Pitjantjatjara. The tallest dome of Kata Tjuta is 546 metres high, which is taller than Uluru. Between the domes are gorges and secluded, deep valleys. The two walking tracks around the domes are The Valley of the Winds Walk and the Walpa Gorge Walk.

Kata Tjuta is an Anangu men's site and is therefore a special place with spiritual significance.

FAST FACT

In 1872, the explorer Ernest Giles found Kata Tjuta, which he named The Olgas.

The Geology of Kata Tjuta

The rocks of Kata Tjuta were harder than those which have weathered away on the surrounding plains, leaving the red domes exposed. Cracks in the great domes then became wider over millions of years, resulting in steep-walled gorges.

Advice for Tourists

The Uluru - Kata Tjuta National Park is in a desert environment. If the temperature rises too high, the walks are closed for public safety. People need to take water with them and to dress appropriately for a walk in a desert.

More Places in the Northern Territory

Karlu Karlu - Devils Marbles

Karlu Karlu - Devils Marbles are large boulders scattered across a valley about 100 kilometres from Tennant Creek. Although they look as though they are about to roll off their ledges, the Karlu Karlu are surprisingly stable. The largest are many metres wide. The shapes of Karlu Karlu were formed by weathering resulting from the effects of extreme heat and cold, rain and wind.

Katherine - Nitmiluk Gorge

The Katherine - Nitmiluk Gorge is in the Nitmiluk National Park, near the town of Katherine and on the traditional land of the Jawoyn people. The gorge is twelve kilometres long and tourists can explore it by hiking or by boat on the Katherine River. The cliffs are red sandstone and are up to seventy metres high. In the wet season, crocodiles move up the river into the park and are captured and relocated by park rangers.

The Jatbula Trail is a long bushwalk starting at the gorge and ending at Edith Falls. The trail passes the beautiful Northern Rockhole, a large pool and waterfall that have been photographed for many promotional campaigns for the area.

Kings Canyon

In the Watarrka National Park, Kings Canyon has high red walls rising above Kings Creek. The traditional custodians are the Luritja Aboriginal people and parts of the canyon are sacred sites. The canyon floor provides a series of microclimates that are a refuge from the heat and arid conditions for many plants and animals. One of these areas, the Garden of Eden, is a permanent waterhole surrounded with thick vegetation and inhabited by a variety of wildlife.

Industries and Business in the Northern Territory

Tourism

The unique World Heritage Sites of Kakadu and Uluru, the largely unspoiled deserts, The Ghan railway journey and the Aboriginal cultural experience all attract tourists to the Northern Territory. Tourism provides employment for many people and is an important contributor to the territory's economy.

Defence Industry

The defence forces have a long history of involvement in the Northern Territory's Top End. Australian combined operations with overseas forces often result in Darwin hosting personnel from the armed forces of other countries.

The defence industry contributes to the Northern Territory economy by providing employment and making use of local businesses. The real estate industry in Darwin is boosted by the presence of large estates there of defence force housing.

Darwin's Defence Support Hub, located near the Robertson Barracks, is an industrial park for businesses that supply and support the Australian Department of Defence.

Commercial Fisheries

Pearl Oyster Fishery

Most pearl oysters used for farming in the Northern Territory are raised in hatcheries. The oysters are collected for pearls, for the oyster meat and for the mother-of-pearl shells.

Barramundi

Wild and farmed barramundi fishing industries operate in the Northern Territory.

Trepang or Sea Cucumber

This aquatic creature was the reason Macassan fishermen travelled to the north coast of Australia from the 1600s onwards. The trepang is still a food delicacy and its harvesting by hand is strictly controlled by government licensing.

Darwin Aquaculture Centre

This centre is investigating aquaculture projects that could benefit Aboriginal communities. Their studies are trialling the farmed production of sea cucumbers, giant clams and oysters.

Mining

Manganese - The large manganese mine on Groote Eylandt has operated since the early 1960s. The mine produces around 15% of the world's manganese. The Anindilyakwa people are the traditional custodians of Groote Eylandt.

Aluminium - Nhulunbuy was established in 1972 as a mining town to house the employees of the bauxite mine on the Gove Peninsula in Arnhem Land. The mine suspended operations in 2014.

Copper - The Northern Territory has large reserves of copper ore, although no mining is currently undertaken.

Diamonds - One of the largest diamonds ever found was mined from the Merlin diamond mine.

Gold - The three largest goldfields in the Northern Territory are at Pine Creek, Tennant Creek and in the Tanami.

Iron Ore - The largest iron ore deposits in the Northern Territory are at Frances Creek, Roper Bar and Mount Peake.

Zinc, Lead, Silver - The McArthur River mine has been a large producer of metal ores.

Natural Gas

Natural gas was first used in the Northern Territory in 1986 when gas from the Amadeus Basin in central Australia was piped into Darwin for electricity generation.

Natural gas is mined throughout the Northern Territory, both onshore and from offshore drilling platforms. Pipelines connect mines with power stations and with an LNG plant near Darwin. The Owen Springs Power Station near Alice Springs is fed by a gas pipeline that runs all the way from the northern coast of the Northern Territory at Wadeye.

Ranger Uranium Mine

Uranium has been mined and processed at the Ranger mine since 1981. The uranium was sold for generating electricity in Asia, Europe and North America. The mine is located near Jabiru and is surrounded by Kakadu National Park. The mine has now ceased operating and rehabilitation of the landscape will involve backfilling the mined area and cleaning the mine's dam.

FAST FACTS

WHAT MAKES URANIUM MINING DIFFERENT?

- The Australian government imposes controls on who can buy uranium
- Buyers must only use uranium for peaceful purposes
- The radioactive mining waste needs special disposal methods

Agriculture and Livestock in the Northern Territory

Forestry

About 47,000 hectares in the Northern Territory are used for plantation forestry. This makes it the second largest land use in the Northern Territory after cattle grazing. Plantation forests currently grow African mahogany, black wattle and sandalwood.

Mangoes

The Katherine region produces most of the Northern Territory's mango crop. The harvest varies annually depending on the weather conditions, but the Northern Territory is becoming one of Australia's leading sources, producing about $62 million worth of mangoes each year.

Fruit and Vegetables

Watermelons, rockmelons and Chinese cabbage are high value agricultural products in the Northern Territory. In 2013, the banana industry was severely affected by a fungus infection which resulted in destruction of crops. This incident reinforces the importance of having strong quarantine measures to protect the agricultural industry.

Cattle

The Port of Darwin is one of the busiest livestock ports in the world. About half the live cattle exported by Australia pass through this port, with the main destinations being Indonesia and South East Asia. Many cattle raised in the Northern Territory are the result of cross-breeding with the Brahman variety of cattle to produce offspring that thrive in the heat and humidity of the Top End.

WORD FILE

quarantine - separating dangerous plants or animals and their diseases

Environment and Sustainability in the Northern Territory

Sustainable practices for agriculture and industry require a balance between using the land and waterways for development and keeping areas as regions of natural beauty. The protection of endangered plants and animals is also important.

Waste Management in Remote Areas

Local government in the Northern Territory has identified a number of challenges for waste disposal in small and remote communities

- Long distances for council workers to travel
- Rocky soils make disposal of ordinary and hazardous waste difficult
- Floods during the monsoon affect all local government activities

RESOURCES	HOW WE CAN LOOK AFTER THEM
SOIL	Correct use of fertilisers and avoiding soil erosion
WATER	Keeping water supplies unpolluted
NATIVE PLANTS	Avoid complete clearing of areas for pastures
NATIVE ANIMALS	Keep some areas of natural bushland for food and shelter
AIR QUALITY	Avoid polluting the air through poor industrial practices

Crocodiles

Saltwater crocodiles live in estuaries, rivers, billabongs and other bodies of water in the north of the Northern Territory. Be Crocwise is a government program to educate people about the need to be vigilant when near any waterway where there may be crocodiles, even in freshwater locations. There are more than 100,000 crocodiles in the Northern Territory and residents in towns can come into contact with them as new suburbs expand into crocodile habitats.

Water

Apart from the dams supplying water to Darwin, there are very few other water storage developments in the Northern Territory. This is due to the flatness of the land and the high evaporation rate. The breeding of disease-carrying mosquitoes in dams would create problems in tropical regions, and this is another reason dams are not common methods of water storage in the Northern Territory.

Some farmers use underground water which is pumped to the surface. The overuse of underground water can cause wetlands and springs fed by the same water source to be affected. The salt level of some underground water can damage soil and crops if it is used for irrigation.

Biosecurity and Quarantine

The Northern Territory restricts the import of the following items as they may contain pests and diseases which could affect local agriculture and livestock:

Fruits and vegetables
Lawn turf
Soil
Seeds and grains
Plants

Animal Pests in the Northern Territory

A feral animal is one which has once been a domestic pet or livestock and has escaped or been released and is now a pest animal. There are many types of feral animals in the Northern Territory. They damage the natural environment and kill native animals. Some of them, such as buffalo and wild pigs, can attack people.

Feral Camels

Although feral camels are now a pest, destroying vegetation with overgrazing and muddying water sources, the camels were once an important asset to the Northern Territory. Thousands of them were imported in the 1800s to help explorers and settlers by providing a freight service with their Afghan cameleer handlers.

WORD FILE

biosecurity - controlling plants, insects and animals that are harmful

sustainability - ability of the environment to be used without being destroyed

Other feral and pest animals not welcome in the Northern Territory

Mammals

cats, goats, buffalo, wild pigs, donkeys, horses, foxes, rabbits, dogs, deer

Non - mammals

cane toads, doves, sparrows, fruit flies, thrips and various mosquitoes, bees, ants

Government of the Northern Territory

Timeline of Government in the Northern Territory

1825 The colony of New South Wales expanded to include the area of the Northern Territory.

1863 South Australia took over responsibility for the Northern Territory.

1888 The whole of the Northern Territory made up just one electorate of the South Australian colonial government.

1911 An Administrator was appointed by the Commonwealth government to manage the Northern Territory.

1947 A partly-elected Legislative Council was formed.

1974 A new, fully-elected Legislative Assembly met in Darwin.

1978 The Northern Territory (Self Government) Act was passed by the Commonwealth government, giving the Northern Territory a status similar to that of the states.

1988 A referendum was held asking voters whether the Northern Territory should become a state. Their answer was that it should remain a Commonwealth territory.

THINK ABOUT IT

Why do you think voters in 1998 did not want the Northern Territory to become a state of Australia?

FAST FACTS

There are four matters over which the Commonwealth government retains the power to legislate for the Northern Territory:

- Uranium mining
- Industrial relations
- Aboriginal land rights
- National parks

Parliament House

The site of Parliament House is where Darwin's post office used to stand. Part of the post office wall was included in the new Parliament House building, as a reminder of the wartime bombing raid in 1942, when the post office and many of Darwin's buildings were destroyed. The new Parliament House was opened in 1994, after Cyclone Tracy destroyed the building that had been on the site since 1955.

WORD FILE

unicameral - a government having one house or section

Local Government

The Northern Territory has 17 local government councils. The first local council in the Northern Territory was the Palmerston District Council in 1874. This later became the Darwin City Council.

The Northern Territory Parliament Today

The Northern Territory has a unicameral government whose head is called the Chief Minister. There are 25 electorates for the territory's Legislative Assembly, some of them with extremely large areas.

The Northern Territory has a Westminster System style of government. The Administrator of the Northern Territory is the local representative of the Governor General of Australia.

FAST FACTS

The annual Northern Territory Australian of the Year Awards honour people who have made an outstanding contribution to the Northern Territory. There are 6 categories:

- Northern Territory Australian of the Year
- Northern Territory Senior Australian
- Northern Territory Young Australian
- Northern Territory Achiever
- Northern Territory Local Hero

Notable People of the Northern Territory

David Gulpilil
David Gulpilil was born in Arnhem Land in 1953. He is an actor and has appeared in the films Storm Boy, The Last Wave, Crocodile Dundee, and Rabbit-Proof Fence. He is also an author of children's books, a singer, an activist for land rights, and a Member of the Order of Australia. David Gulpilil is a Yolngu man.

Paul Everingham
Paul Everingham was the first Chief Minister of the newly independent government of the Northern Territory. He served in this position from 1978 to 1984. He then ran for election in the Federal Parliament, and served the Northern Territory in the Australian House of Representatives from 1984 to 1987.

Rosalie Kunoth-Monks
Rosalie Kunoth-Monks was born at the Utopia Cattle Station in the Northern Territory in 1937. She featured in the movie Jedda, which was the first Australian movie made in colour. Rosalie Kunoth-Monks later became an Anglican nun. She left the order to work for indigenous welfare and education, and to become an activist for indigenous rights. Rosalie Kunoth-Monks is an Anmatyerre woman.

Jessica Mauboy
Jessica Mauboy was born in Darwin in 1989. After her singing performances in 2006 on the TV talent show, Australian Idol, Jessica Mauboy has pursued a professional career. Her albums have achieved gold and platinum status, and her work has also been recognised with ARIA and Deadly Awards. Her acting career includes roles in the films Bran Nue Day and The Sapphires. In 2014, she sang in the Eurovision Song Contest, which was broadcast around the world.

Mandawuy Yunupingu
Mandawuy Yunupingu was born in Arnhem Land in 1956. He was the principal of the Yirrkala Community School until 1991. He then decided to concentrate on his music and helped to found the band, Yothu Yindi. In 1992, Mandawuy Yunupingu was made Australian of the Year for his work in improving understanding amongst Australians. He died in 2013.

Clyde Fenton
Clyde Fenton was born in 1901. He was the first doctor to provide medical services by aircraft in the Northern Territory. In the 1930s, he operated the Northern Territory Aerial Medical Service, flying his own Gypsy Moth aircraft. He also worked with the Flying Doctor Service. Clyde Fenton died in 1982.

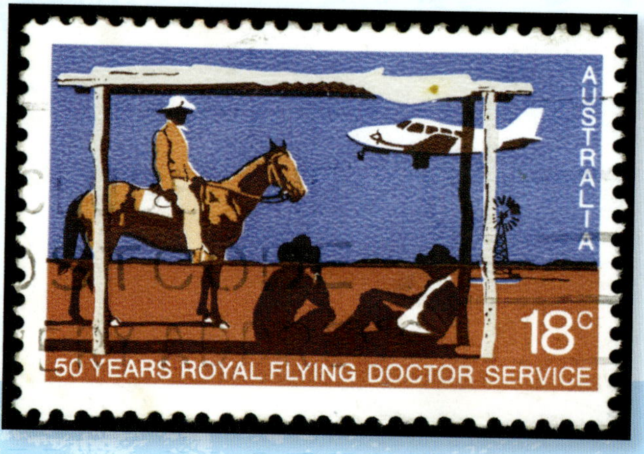

Emily Kame Kngwarreye

Emily Kame Kngwarreye was born in the Northern Territory in about 1910. One of the leading women artists of the dot painting style in Australia, Emily Kngwarreye started painting late in her life and did not receive international fame until she was in her eighties. Her deeply spiritual art concentrates on women's Dreaming subjects, representing her land, food sources and Dreamtime stories. She was an Anmatyerre Elder and she died in 1996.

Albert Namatjira

Albert Namatjira was born in Hermannsburg, Northern Territory in 1902. He was the first Aboriginal artist to receive acclaim from art critics. His watercolour landscapes of desert scenes are painted in the European style of the time. Although western art reviewers saw his landscapes as representations of the natural beauty of the subject, Namatjira was also painting his traditional lands using his detailed knowledge of their spiritual significance. Albert Namatjira was an Arrernte man and he died in 1959.

Clifford Possum Tjapaltjarri

Clifford Possum Tjapaltjarri was born on Napperby Station, Northern Territory in about 1932. He was a leading figure in the Papunya Artists group and helped develop the dot painting style into an art movement that received worldwide attention. One of his paintings sold at an auction in 2007 for $2.4 million. He was awarded an Order of Australia in 2002, but passed away before receiving it.

Leisel Jones

Leisel Jones is a Olympic gold medallist in swimming. She was born in Katherine in 1985 and competed in her first Olympic Games in 2000, when she was only fifteen years old. She won her individual gold medal for the 100 metres breaststroke at the Beijing Olympics in 2008, winning by a whole body length. At the same Olympics she was also part of the women's gold medal winning relay team for the 100 metre medley.

Cadel Evans

Cadel Evans was born in Katherine in 1977. He is a former racing cyclist and won the Tour de France cycling race in 2011. Evans retired from racing in 2015.

Vincent Lingiari

Vincent Lingiari was born at Victoria River Gorge, Northern Territory in 1919. In 1966, he led a strike in protest against poor wages and conditions on the cattle station that employed men of the Gurindji people. The strikers also wanted their land returned to them so that they could manage their own cattle station. In 1974, Prime Minister Whitlam returned land at Wave Hill to the Gurindji people. Vincent Lingiari received the Order of Australia in 1976. He died in 1988.

Flags, Symbols, Emblems and Special Days of the Northern Territory

People living in the Northern Territory use flags, symbols and special days to show their connection to their community. These connections include pride for the group they belong to, an interest in the history of their group or area, and wanting to join others for celebrations that bring people together.

Northern Territory Flag

The Northern Territory flag dates from 1978 when it was first flown to celebrate self-government for the Northern Territory. The flag was designed by Robert Ingpen.

- The five stars represent the Southern Cross constellation.
- The flower represents Sturt's desert rose, the floral emblem of the Northern Territory.
- The three official colours of the Northern Territory are black, white and red ochre.

Australian Aboriginal Flag

The Aboriginal Flag was first flown in 1971. It was designed by Elder Harold Thomas.
Yellow disc - the sun and yellow ochre
Red - the land
Black - the Aboriginal people of Australia

Special Days

Australia Day - On 26th January each year, Australians commemorate the 1788 founding of a British colony by Governor Phillip at Sydney Cove.
ANZAC Day - Ceremonies and marches for ANZAC Day are held all around Australia on 25th April each year.
NAIDOC Week - A week in July each year to celebrate the history, culture and achievements of Aboriginal and Torres Strait Islander peoples. Communities and government bodies organise events around the Northern Territory for NAIDOC Week.

RULES FOR FLYING THESE FLAGS

- **Don't fly more than one on the same pole.**
- **Don't fly them in the dark.**
- **Raise the flag to the top of the pole before lowering it to half-mast.**
- **Treat these flags with respect.**

Special Days Only Held in the Northern Territory

Territory Day is held on 1st July each year to celebrate the granting of self-government to the Northern Territory in 1978.

Picnic Day is held on the first Monday of August each year.

Agricultural show days are held in Alice Springs, Tennant Creek, Katherine, Darwin and Borroloola.

Symbols of the Northern Territory

Floral Emblem - Sturt's desert rose
Animal Emblem - Red kangaroo
Bird Emblem - Wedge-tailed eagle

The Coat of Arms

The Coat of Arms is a symbol of the Northern Territory and each part of it has a meaning.

Sturt's desert rose is the floral emblem of the Northern Territory.
The red kangaroo and the wedge-tailed eagle are the animal and bird emblems of the Northern Territory.
The shield is decorated with Aboriginal art showing a woman and paths connecting camp sites.
The kangaroos hold shells found in the waters along the coast of the Northern Territory.
The eagle holds an Aboriginal Tjurunga ritual stone.
The helmet refers to the defence history of the Northern Territory.

WORD FILE

Elder - a respected Aboriginal person who is a custodian of traditional knowledge
half-mast - flying a flag halfway up the pole as a mark of respect when a community leader dies

Make Your Own Coat of Arms

Design a Coat of Arms for your family, suburb or sport group, etc.

- Use symbols that everyone will know
- Your own Coat of Arms could include drawings or pictures to tell the history of the group
- Think about where to use your Coat of Arms
- What language will you use for a motto?
- Where have you seen the NT Coat of Arms used?

How to Find Out More

Primary and Secondary Sources

There are many ways to find out more about the Northern Territory. You can do this using both primary and secondary sources. Websites can have a mixture of both types of sources on them.

Primary Sources

Interviews - when people say what they have seen
Letters - when the writer was the person experiencing the event
Newspapers - when the facts are presented
Photos - when they have not been altered
Maps
Old Items & Antiques
News on Television - when it shows pictures of real events
School Newsletters - when they list names or dates of events
Videos on Youtube or Facebook - when they show an event and have not been altered

Secondary Sources

- **Letters** - when the writer is retelling the facts that someone else told them
- **Newspapers** - when the story is told by someone who retells the facts that someone else told them
- **Photos** - when the photo has been altered
- **Songs, Poems, Stories**
- **News on Television** - when it is reported by a journalist who did not experience the event

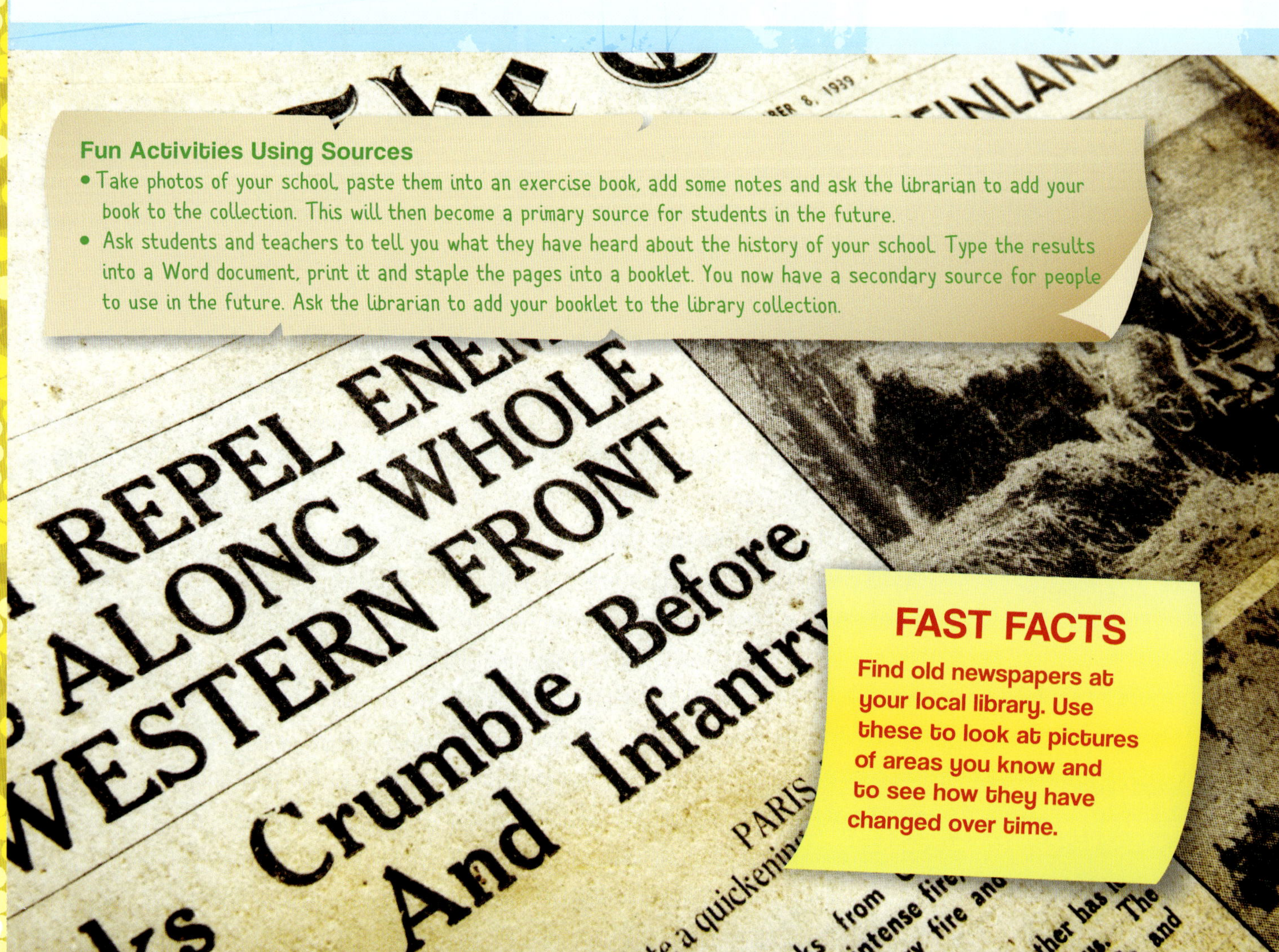

Fun Activities Using Sources

- Take photos of your school, paste them into an exercise book, add some notes and ask the librarian to add your book to the collection. This will then become a primary source for students in the future.
- Ask students and teachers to tell you what they have heard about the history of your school. Type the results into a Word document, print it and staple the pages into a booklet. You now have a secondary source for people to use in the future. Ask the librarian to add your booklet to the library collection.

FAST FACTS

Find old newspapers at your local library. Use these to look at pictures of areas you know and to see how they have changed over time.

Museums in the Northern Territory

The historic objects in museums are primary sources. Looking at these objects gives us an insight into how people lived in the past.

- Museum and Art Gallery of the Northern Territory, Darwin
- Defence of Darwin Experience, Darwin
- Museum of Central Australia, Alice Springs
- Fannie Bay Gaol, Darwin
- Katherine Museum, Katherine
- Darwin Military Museum, Darwin

FAST FACT

The Museum and Art Gallery of the Northern Territory has hosted the National Aboriginal and Torres Strait Islander Art Award since 1984.

Your Own Family and Friends

Primary sources do not always have to be about famous people. Interviews with your family and friends are important too. Your grandmother might recall what your suburb used to be like. Friends can share stories about coming to live in the Northern Territory, either from other parts of Australia or from a country overseas.

Websites

Find more information about the Northern Territory on these websites:

- www.australiasnorthernterritory.com.au
- www.nt.gov.au

Glossary

biosecurity - controlling plants, insects and animals that are harmful
colonise - to settle in a new land and impose a new culture on the people living there
contemporary - modern
Elder - a respected Aboriginal person who is a custodian of traditional knowledge
escarpments - cliffs at the edge of a plateau
half-mast - flying a flag halfway up the pole as a mark of respect when a community leader dies
microclimate - the climate in a very small area
quarantine - separating dangerous plants or animals and their diseases
sustainability - ability of the environment to be used without being destroyed
traditional ownership - the Aboriginal land ownership system
unicameral - a government having one house or section

Index

www.redbackpublishing.com.au